IMAGES
*of America*

# SOUTHAMPTON

The sign that stood for many decades at the western entrance to Southampton Village.

IMAGES
*of America*

# SOUTHAMPTON

Mary Cummings

ARCADIA

First published 1996
Copyright © Mary Cummings, 1996

ISBN 0-7524-0459-8

Published by Arcadia Publishing,
an imprint of the Chalford Publishing Corporation
One Washington Center, Dover, New Hampshire 03820
Printed in Great Britain

*This book is dedicated to
Elizabeth H. Johnson*

The Ponquogue Lighthouse, built in 1857, demolished in 1948.

# Contents

# Acknowledgments

In addition to the help we received from historical associations and others whose collections are credited, we are grateful for cooperation of the Meadow Club, the National Golf Links of America, the Shinnecock Golf Club, and the Southampton Bathing Corporation. And we especially appreciate the generosity of those individuals who shared their family photographs, reminiscences, and history with us. Our thanks to: Karen Adelwerth, Vivian Carle, Karl and Janet Grossman, Richard G. Hendrickson, Robert Keene, Harry Martin, Douglas Morris, Laura Race, Ethel Schmitt, Faruk Yorgancioglu, and Martha Siedlecki.

# Introduction

Southampton, rich in history and scenic beauty, is one of ten towns in Suffolk County, New York. Situated on the south shore of eastern Long Island, it was settled in 1640 by a small band of English Puritans who had obtained permission from the Earl of Stirling "to sitt downe upon Long Island . . . there to possess improve and enjoy eight miles square of land." When they arrived by boat from Lynn, Massachusetts, they found fertile soil, fish-filled waters, beautiful vistas, and a generally friendly Native American population that had preceded them by thousands of years.

The Shinnecock, whose tribe was one of thirteen on Long Island in 1640, shared their survival skills with the Europeans. With their help, the settlers weathered the first difficult years and prepared the way for Southampton's eventual expansion to its present dimensions: 109,530 acres (89,570 of land and 19,960 of water) with a total of 658 miles of waterfront. Within its borders, the town encompasses five incorporated villages—Southampton, Sag Harbor, North Haven, Quogue and Westhampton Beach—and more than a dozen hamlets, each with its own distinct character.

During the summer months, Southampton's year-round population of approximately 46,000 swells as much as threefold, but despite its reputation as a resort of international renown, the town remains remarkable for its open spaces and farmland, for the new England flavor of its village streets, and for its many visible links with the past. Among them, at the place where the original families first stepped ashore, is a boulder that bears the inscription: "Near this spot in June 1640 landed colonists from Lynn, Massachusetts who founded Southampton, the first English settlement in New York State."

During the Colonial era Southampton maintained strong ties to New England, which was easily reached by boat, while the 90-mile trip to Manhattan via stagecoach took more than two days. At home, daily life followed agrarian rhythms, town business was conducted in the meeting house, and Puritan morality was written into the town's legal code by the colony's Calvinist minister. While farming was the colonists' principal occupation, fishing was also important and by 1650 the first commercial whaling company had been formed. Because Long Island was lost to the British near the start of the Revolutionary War, local military activity was minimal but the hardships of enemy occupation were considerable, causing some families to flee to Connecticut.

Even before independence, Sag Harbor, a village that never fit the agrarian pattern, had developed a thriving coastal and foreign trade and by 1789 its port was busier than New York

City's. During the golden age of the whaling industry, which peaked in Sag Harbor between 1837 and 1847, there were more than fifty ships in the harbor fleet and the mansions built for their wealthy owners brought a new elegance to village streets. With its urbane architecture, its crowds of exotic foreigners, and its lively taverns, the village of Sag Harbor was the exception in a town in which the century following the Revolutionary War was marked by normal growth in relative isolation from the rest of the world.

The arrival of the Long Island Rail Road around 1870 ushered in a new era. New Yorkers and others, who could now reach the town's charming villages and unspoiled beaches in a few hours, at first sought lodging in boarding houses, then built their own sprawling summer cottages. By the turn of the century, Southampton was ranked among the most fashionable resorts on the East Coast and was undergoing rapid physical changes. Between 1895 and 1913 a host of impressive new public buildings went up in the villages, not a few of them conceived and financed by wealthy summer residents who took it upon themselves to fill perceived cultural gaps. It was also during this period that Southampton acquired its fabled golf links, private clubs, and many of its lavish estates.

This heady activity was reined in when the first federal income tax in 1913 was followed almost immediately by World War I. When the good times returned, it was less common—though not unknown—for summer residents to arrive for the season accompanied by ten or more servants. But if defenders of the town's puritanical heritage, who had waged a relentless temperance campaign in the local press, hoped for a return to the old ways when Prohibition was passed in 1919, they were disappointed. Instead, speakeasies came to Southampton, as did rumrunners and others whose lawlessness went largely unpunished. Automobiles also arrived in increasing numbers, bringing glamour to village streets which were taking on a decidedly twentieth-century look. The Great Depression, which hit Southampton somewhat later than elsewhere and was cushioned for farm families by the availability of food, was effectively ended by the terrible hurricane of 1938, which put many people to work rebuilding.

World War II put progress on hold once again in Southampton as patriotic duty summoned men to serve in Europe and the Pacific while women assumed extra tasks on the home front. When it was over, life resumed its normal rhythms, though from the fifties onward the pace of development would be ever-accelerating.

# One

# A Place
# Frozen in Time

*Once Southampton's original settlers had survived the first harsh winters following their arrival in 1640, life in the town remained practically unchanged for more than two centuries. Farming, fishing, and whaling were the principal occupations; horses provided the power.*

Montauk Highway, Bridgehampton, in the 1890s. The carriage is passing the present site of the post office. (Bridge Hampton Historical Society Collection.)

The Halsey House on South Main Street, Southampton Village, at the turn of the century. In 1648, the whole Southampton colony moved from Olde Towne, near the present site of Southampton Hospital, to Towne Street (Main Street today), where every householder was allotted a "home lott." Recognized as the earliest English frame house in New York State, the house built by Thomas Halsey in 1648 still stands and is open seasonally to visitors as a museum. (Southampton Historical Museum Collection.)

The Hildreth House in Mecox, built around 1690 and torn down around 1873. "Saltboxes" were generally set facing south, sometimes using a compass so that at high noon the sun was in direct line with the house frame. By setting markers on the north side of the house, it was possible to tell the hour from the position of the shadow cast by the house, which served as a giant sundial. The south roof was short, and the north so low as to leave only room enough for a door under the eaves.

The old Pelletreau House in Southampton Village, built in 1686. Houses were plain in Colonial days and windows were neither many nor large since glass was heavily taxed and expensive. The 3-foot cedar shingles went without paint. Built by Stephen Boyer, the house and shop were later occupied by Southampton's celebrated goldsmith, silversmith, and Revolutionary War patriot, Captain Elias Pelletreau (1726–1810). The house was torn down around 1878 but the shop survives as a museum.

The Herrick House in earlier days. Built in 1751, the house on North Main Street in Southampton Village was used by troops serving under General Erskine, commander of the British occupation forces in the Revolutionary War. While there were no important military operations in the town, occupation by the enemy following the Battle of Long Island defeat in 1776 deprived many families of their homes and livelihoods. Some sought refuge in Connecticut, returning afterwards to find their properties in desuetude or destroyed. (Morris Studio Collection.)

Plowing the Hildreth farm in Southampton Village. The horse-drawn plow was a familiar sight in Southampton for almost three centuries.

The Hildreth farm on Toylsome Lane before the turn of the century. Thomas Hildreth, who was among the first group of settlers arriving in Southampton between 1640 and 1642, had two sons: Joseph, the elder, who got most of the Southampton property; and James, who moved to Bridgehampton. The Toylsome Lane property was farmed into the twentieth century. From the cupola the view was across farm fields to the Atlantic, where the passage of tall-masted ships could be monitored.

The *Benjamin B. Church*. In the era of the great sailing ships, scanners of the Atlantic watching from cupolas and rooftops might have counted as many as six masts on the majestic vessels that plied the coastal waters carrying cargo. It was perilous work and shipwrecks were far from uncommon off the shores of Southampton. On April 7, 1894, the three-masted schooner *Benjamin B. Church*, carrying coal, met its end at Mecox. Eight crewmen were saved but the vessel was a total loss. (Southampton Historical Museum Collection.)

A typical early life saving station. Until well into the present century, Southampton men were predominantly farmer-fishermen and were often as at home on the water as in the field. Before 1848, when the U.S. Life Saving Service (later the Coast Guard) was created, rescues along the coast were made by volunteers, many of them expert whalers. In 1871, the life saving stations were reorganized and made more professional. (Southampton Historical Museum Collection.)

Ponquogue Lighthouse (sometimes called Shinnecock Lighthouse), in 1898. Until this lighthouse went into service on January 1, 1858, Montauk Lighthouse, erected in 1796, was the only one on eastern Long Island. Several shipwrecks in the years immediately following its inauguration were thought to have resulted from confusion over the change. In the days before ocean telegraphy, there was no way of communicating navigational alterations to crews at sea. (Southampton Historical Museum Collection.)

The crew of the Quogue Life Saving Station with wreckage from the *Nahum Chapin* in a January 21, 1899, photograph. At the far left is Bill Halsey; second from the left is Ed Warner; third from the left is Frank Warner. Others include: Captain Al Jackson, Wren Overton, and Ambrose Rowley. The small coastal schooner *Nahum Chapin* had been beached two years earlier, on January 21, 1897, during a winter storm. The vessel and its crew of eleven were lost. (Quogue Historical Society Collection.)

Wickham Cuffee (1826-1915). One of eight children born to Sarah Bunn and Vincent Cuffee of the Shinnecock Reservation, Wickham Cuffee spent many years as a whaler and made many friends in Southampton.

A painting of Sag Harbor in whaling days. Whaling was first mentioned in the town records in 1648 when regulations for the disposition of whales cast up on shore were drawn up. The Native Americans, who had been practicing a form of on-shore whaling long before that date, shared their skills with the settlers, a few of whom formed a company to go out to sea in pursuit of whales as early as 1650. During the golden era of whaling—1820–1850, the period portrayed in this painting—Sag Harbor had more than sixty-three whaling vessels in its fleet and was a rival of Salem and New Bedford as a major whaling port. The last whaling voyage out of Sag Harbor took place in 1871. (Southampton Town Historian Collection.)

The last of the whaling men on parade in 1907. To celebrate the bicentennial of Sag Harbor in 1907, the village held a parade in which the last of the whalers passed in review aboard a whaling boat. Among them were: Frank Wadel, William Roben, Ed Bill, Manuel Silvey, and George Page. (John Jermain Library Collection.)

16

Sag Harbor, *c.* 1900. At the turn of the century, Sag Harbor was struggling for an economic foothold in a world that no longer needed whale oil. The decline had been precipitous from the days when the village wharves and streets were crowded with exotic foreign sailors, wealthy shipowners in "long-tailed coats and plug hats," and all kinds of colorful characters. In 1875, just four years after the last whaling voyage left Sag Harbor, a writer described it as, "one deserted village, a seaport from which all life had disappeared." The discovery of gold in California, of petroleum in Pennsylvania, and a scarcity of whales had all contributed to the decline. Among the various enterprises that came in to restore vitality to Sag Harbor's streets in the latter part of the nineteenth century, Joseph Fahys's watchcase factory was probably the most significant. Arriving in 1881, it was well established by 1900 when this shot of Main Street, Sag Harbor, was taken. (Southampton Town Historian Collection.)

Dr. Edgar B. Mulford in front of his house on Lumber Lane, Bridgehampton. Well-known throughout eastern Long Island, Dr. Mulford was born in Amagansett in 1848, graduated from Bellevue Medical College in the early 1870s, and continued to make his rounds in and around Bridgehampton until the day he died while preparing for his afternoon consultations. The house still stands at the south end of the street. (Bridge Hampton Historical Society Collection.)

Dr. George Horace Hallock, *c.* 1870. Southampton Village's first doctor was practicing in the North Fork community of Laurel when he was "called" to Southampton, which was without a physician. He built a house on South Main Street and the family remained in Southampton where his grandson, David Horace Hallock, also became a prominent doctor.

The Old Schoolhouse in Quogue in the early 1880s. Churches were the first priority for the early settlers, but schools ran a close second. Well-educated for their time, Southampton's founders hired a schoolmaster to teach village children soon after appointing a minister, Abraham Pierson, in 1640. In Quogue, settled some ten years later, the earliest written record of schooling is a 1795 list of scholars. The first schoolhouse was completed in 1822. Looking northeast from approximately the head of Old Depot Road, the schoolhouse (at left) can be seen in its original location on Quogue Road. The homes of John H. Post (center), and Henry Gardiner (at right), were both boarding houses. (Quogue Library Collection.)

The North End School in Bridgehampton, *c.* 1895. The Brennan sisters are among the pupils pictured. Elizabeth Brennan is at the far left and Johanna and Veronica Brennan are third and fourth from the left, respectively.

The Brennan farm in Mecox in 1905. Mary and Patrick Brennan immigrated from England in the 1890s, stopping first at Greenport and then moving on to Mecox. The Brennans' daughter, Elizabeth, is the girl on the right. At Elizabeth's right is Florence Halsey.

Elizabeth Brennan and Florence Halsey on the Brennan farm in Mecox in 1905.

The Beebe Windmill in Bridgehampton on February 12, 1899. Built in 1820 in Sag Harbor, the Beebe mill was moved at least three times before arriving at its current location on Ocean Road. Plans to move it to Brooklyn's Prospect Park were abandoned, however, because of the difficulty of transporting it the length of Long Island. This view shows the mill when it was located near the railroad tracks and operated by the Bridgehampton Milling Company. (Ron Ziel Collection.)

The south end of Lake Agawam in the 1890s. Coaches, buggies, and horse-drawn carriages of all descriptions took people to and from the beaches of Southampton Village. (Southampton Historical Museum Collection.)

Delivery wagons in Southampton Village in the 1890s. The Gardner Bakery wagon (shown at right) shared the roads with countless others laden with goods for Southampton's households and businesses. (Southampton Historical Museum Collection.)

A construction site in Southampton Village at the turn of the century. Men and horses labored together at this site located only a stone's throw from the Presbyterian Church at the corner of Main Street and Jobs Lane. (Southampton Historical Museum Collection.)

Southampton's Presbyterian Church, prior to 1890. Completed in 1843, the church, which still serves the village, was the fourth since the settlers founded the first church in 1640. The first church was a rude thatched building that served also as school, courthouse, and town meeting hall. The second was built in 1652/3 on South Main Street. These churches, as well as the third, built in 1707, were for the whole community, as church and state were one in the early days of the colony. Documents expressly stated, however, that the new building was to be used by those Protestants usually known as Presbyterians—the first time the word Presbyterian was attached to any church in the Province of New York. The present structure was completed in 1843 and a chapel was added in 1895. (Southampton Historical Museum Collection.)

The Bishop general store and post office in Westhampton in the late nineteenth century. In its day, Bishop's, at Mill Road near Baycrest Avenue, was a true country store, providing for almost every need and housing the local post office as well. It was clearly a popular gathering spot. (Westhampton Beach Historical Society Collection.)

Tea merchant John Bradshaw with his delivery wagon in Bridgehampton at the turn of the century. Mr. Bradshaw lived with his family in a house on Montauk Highway that stood where the Allan Schneider real estate building is now. (Bridge Hampton Historical Society Collection.)

John L. Cook (1850–1909) and his mother, Hannah H. Cook, seated, c. 1905. This photograph was taken at the Cook homestead on Mecox Road west of Horse Mill Lane in Bridgehampton. The house was later occupied by Lawrence C. Halsey. (Bridge Hampton Historical Society Collection.)

Spring flooding, *c.* 1900. Once a marsh, the Windmill Lane-Jobs Lane area of Southampton Village used to flood fairly frequently and still can be swampy at times, though now it is mostly covered with concrete. Here, a coach from the fleet of Charles R. Fitz carries passengers across the water in front of J. M. Jagger's carpentry shop. (Southampton Town Historian Collection.)

South Main Street, Southampton Village. They came by carriage, bicycle, and on horseback to see the fox on South Main Street *c.* 1900. (Southampton Town Historian Collection.)

Boating on Jobs Lane *c.* 1900. While the men relied on their Wellingtons to stay dry, the ladies found a better way to cross the watery road. In the prow, front and center, is Mary Hallock. (Southampton Town Historian Collection.)

*Moonlight on Shinnecock Bay at Walker House, East Quogue, L. I.*

A peaceful scene at Walker House in East Quogue, *c.* 1900. The oak branch bower, predecessor to the beach umbrella, was once a common sight on beaches throughout the town. (East Quogue Historical Society Collection.)

*Vail House, East Quogue, L.I.*
*John Hauser, Prop.*
*Duck & Broiler Dinners a specialty*

The Vail House in East Quogue, *c.* 1900. A favorite with local residents, gunners, and summer visitors, the Vail House was a popular spot all year. (East Quogue Historical Society Collection.)

Jackson House at Achabacawesuck Creek in East Quogue at the turn of the century. The house, which is unoccupied but still stands, is said to be the oldest in East Quogue. (East Quogue Historical Society Collection.)

The footbridge over Achabacawesuck Creek, *c.* 1900. It was not until much later that Montauk Highway became the main east-west thoroughfare through East Quogue. At the turn of the century only foot traffic crossed the creek, whose Native American name means "spring cold water stream." (East Quogue Historical Society Collection.)

29

Main Street in Westhampton Beach at the turn of the century. In this photograph, a horse-drawn produce delivery wagon shares the road with an automobile. The overlap would last for years on eastern Long Island, where people were especially reluctant to give up their horses. In many places, sidewalks were paved before roads, and even those who owned automobiles were apt to hitch up the buggy instead. (Westhampton Beach Historical Society Collection.)

A summer day on Sag Pond, Sagaponack, in 1870. There are few clues in this scene to indicate that it dates back more than one hundred years. (Southampton Historical Museum Collection.)

The beach at Sagaponack, c. 1905. As practical as umbrellas in providing protection from the sun, oak branch arbors like the one on the left were lovely to look at and required no dismantling at the end of the season. A storm could be counted on to do the job. (Southampton Historical Museum Collection.)

The Southampton town football team on October 16, 1897. James Augustus ("Gus") Hildreth, seated with the ball, captained this team which he was instrumental in organizing at a time when rules for the new game were still being formulated. An avid athlete, he inherited the family farm on Toylsome Lane and served for eighteen years as town supervisor but never lost his interest in sports. Other members of the team, which was photographed at the Josiah Foster house in Southampton Village, were, from left to right: (standing) Hubert Squires, Harry Stevens, Frank Burnett, Henry Schwenk, Mr. Goodale, Mr. Martin, Ted Moeran, and Will Bennett; (kneeling) Bev Daley, Will Fordham, E. Howell, and Mac Benedict; (sitting) Will Halsey, Lewis Squires, Gus Hildreth, Arthur Daley, and Mr. Evans.

A Southampton Village street around the turn of the century. It is not known what brought this crowd of dapper men interspersed with a few women and children to downtown Southampton Village. (Southampton Historical Museum Collection.)

The corner of Main Street and Meeting House Lane, Southampton Village, c. 1900. The crowd appears to be gathered for a Fourth of July parade. (Southampton Historical Museum Collection.)

William Woolley Bishop, c. 1890. From his privileged position, baby William surveyed the scene at the south end of Main Street in Southampton Village. Behind him, at right, is the Captain Rogers home, which was built on the east side of Main Street in 1843 with profits gained from the whaling trade. It was purchased in 1899 by the village's prominent benefactor Samuel L. Parrish, who was also one of the area's early real estate speculators. He moved the house back to its present location, where it is maintained by the Southampton Colonial Society as an historical museum. Also visible, at left, is the village's third church. Erected in 1707, the church was abandoned by the Presbyterians in 1843 and used by the Methodists from 1845 to 1883. In adulthood, William Bishop was one of several colorful butchers who always wore boaters to work at Schwenk's Market on Main Street. (Southampton Town Historian Collection.)

Children in Southampton Village, *c.* 1900. Presumably it was ice cream these well-dressed children were sampling on a summer day in Southampton. (Southampton Town Historian Collection.)

Albert Post at home, *c.* 1900. Albert J. Post was the first "president" of Southampton Village and filled the office from 1894 to 1901. He taught school in 1853 and 1854; was elected town clerk in 1858; and served as town trustee for more than forty years. He was elected town assessor in 1894 and served the community in that capacity until his death in 1907. (Southampton Historical Museum Collection.)

"Ludlow Grange" in Bridgehampton before 1900. This house, on the north side of Montauk Highway east of downtown Bridgehampton, was built in 1880 by Captain Isaac Ludlow (1807–1871), who first went to sea at the age of fifteen and made twenty voyages on whaling ships (eight of them as commander of his vessel) before he retired in about 1857. Rewarded with a fortune that enabled him to build this imposing residence, he also earned the gratitude of the British Admiralty for having rescued 105 of the passengers and crew of a British bark that was wrecked in the Indian Ocean in 1835. The house still stands and is occupied by Southampton Town Historian Robert Keene. (Southampton Town Historian Collection.)

A view of Jobs Lane in Southampton Village, *c.* 1890. This photograph was taken looking east toward the Presbyterian Church. After the Soldiers' and Sailors' Monument was completed in 1902, this site became known as Monument Square. (Southampton Historical Museum Collection.)

36

The George Bascom boathouse on Horse Mill Lane in Bridgehampton in 1896. George Bascom is shown with "Georgie" (whose mother was Sarah Tyson) at the boathouse on Mecox Bay. The estate also featured a carriage house/stable and a hen house for prize fowl. (Bridge Hampton Historical Society Collection.)

Lake Avenue in Southampton, 1880. It is not hard to imagine the enthusiasm of first-time visitors for the scenes of remarkable pastoral beauty which the eastern Long Island villages, relatively isolated due to their geographical remoteness, preserved long after others had lost it. (Southampton Historical Museum Collection.)

# Two

# Emergence from Isolation

*First the railroad was extended to eastern Long Island c. 1870, then the automobile began to take over the roads. Easier access made Southampton's quaint villages and unspoiled beaches popular destinations for city people and the unpretentious resorts favored by early arrivals grew ever-more fashionable after the turn of the century. Boarding houses gave way to big summer "cottages," then to mansions. In Sag Harbor, when plentiful petroleum cut demand for whale oil and the golden age of whaling ended, local leaders turned to manufacturing as an alternative. Immigrants—some lured by jobs, others by farmland—came to stay, while the affluent swelled the town's seasonal population.*

Horse meets iron horse on Butter Lane in Bridgehampton. (Ron Ziel Collection.)

"Mocomanto" (the Frederic H. Betts house) and the family's gondola on Lake Agawam, c. 1882. Considered the jewel of Southampton Village, the lake became a hub of summer activity a century ago and was soon surrounded by handsome houses, ringed with bicycle paths, and dotted with boats sailing south to the beach and back. Certainly the most spectacular

among them was the craft Mrs. Betts had shipped back after a trip to Venice. Every Sunday, poled by the family's four footmen, the gondola crossed the lake to deliver the lady of the house to morning services at St. Andrews Church on the dunes. Mocomanto was the name of a Native American who signed the original deed with the settlers in 1640.

The south end of Lake Agawam in the early 1900s. The dock and the Dune Church for which Mrs. Frederic H. Betts headed every Sunday in her gondola are on the left. Her house is the one at the far right. The nave of the church was originally a life saving station, built in 1851 by the U.S. government. It was bought by Dr. T. Gaillard Thomas and presented to the church in 1879. Called at first Saint Andrews-by-the-Sea, the church was renamed Saint Andrews Dune Church in 1884. (Southampton Historical Museum Collection.)

The south end of Lake Agawam in the early 1900s. Across the lake from the Betts house a simple pavilion was used by bathers and boaters. Bathers could cross the road and swim in the ocean or take a dip in the lake. In 1965, an old-timer described the scene on the lake in that earlier era as "a busy and gay sight as people rowed or sailed down to the beach for a swim." Bicycle paths ran parallel to walking paths around the lake, attracting biking enthusiasts of all ages. (Southampton Historical Museum Collection.)

Gin Lane looking southwest across Lake Agawam in the early 1900s. Seen from where the road curves toward the ocean, this view shows the public ocean bathing station at the far left, a life saving station, the Dune Church, and the houses that were beginning to line the shores of the Atlantic and Lake Agawam. (Southampton Historical Museum Collection.)

Dr. T. Gaillard Thomas's house on the dunes in Southampton Village, c. 1890. Dr. Thomas, who built the first house on the dunes in Southampton in 1877, encouraged his patients to seek out Southampton's salubrious air. To accommodate them, he convinced the Hildreth family to expand their farmhouse on Toylsome Lane, which became one of the first summer boarding houses. His own beach house, known as "The Birdhouse" because its wrap-around porches made it look like a canary cage, was eventually claimed by the sea in a hurricane. (Southampton Historical Museum Collection.)

*The Shinnecock* and *The Greenport* docked in Sag Harbor, *c.* 1903. The extension of the railroad to the South Fork of Long Island from 1869 onward actually finished what the fleet of "White Boats" run by the Montauk Steamboat Company had already started. It was the steam-powered ship that first opened the town to the tourist trade and the railroad that transformed its villages

and hamlets into popular summer resorts. Concerned by the competition, the Long Island Rail Road bought out the steamboat company in 1898 and operated the fleet until the 1920s. (Ron Ziel Collection.)

*The Shinnecock* in Sag Harbor waters, *c.* 1905. The sidewheeler sailed the Sag Harbor-New York route. In addition to travelers bound for New York City, excursionists also enjoyed cruises to Connecticut and back and special holiday sails. (Ron Ziel Collection.)

Children survey the waterfront scene in Sag Harbor, *c.* 1905. (Ron Ziel Collection.)

Southampton station in September 1878. Chartered in 1834, the Long Island Rail Road was determined not to overspend on its stations during the early decades of its operations. Even elegant seasonal visitors who traveled with steamer trunks full of summer finery were obliged to seek shelter in the "basic box." Those in Southampton, Sag Harbor, and Westhampton were identical in appearance. A later wave of station-building in the first decade of the twentieth century replaced all three stations with large, handsome masonry buildings. (Ron Ziel Collection.)

Sag Harbor station on August 4, 1878. Erected at the end of the Sag Harbor line, this station was almost demolished in 1882 when an engineer mistook a light on a steamboat for a railroad signal and overshot the mark. (Ron Ziel Collection.)

A rotary snowplow in Bridgehampton, 1898. In November 1898, the Long Island Rail Road purchased a brand new steam rotary snowplow. On the 28th of that month an early blizzard hit and the plow went to work. (Ron Ziel Collection.)

The Hildreth house on Toylsome Lane in Southampton Village, *c.* 1890. When Dr. T. Gaillard Thomas, a prominent New York City physician, persuaded the Hildreths to enlarge their farmhouse to provide summer lodging for some of his patients, he began a trend. In the 1880s and 1890s boarding houses flourished in the town, as this view of the Hildreth establishment, taken from the other side of a still-unpaved Toylsome Lane, attests. The rocking chairs lined up along the front porch are all occupied and even the porch roof serves as a perch. While a pair of horses waits for them to return to their carriage, a young couple, their child seated atop the gatepost, poses jauntily for a family portrait.

The Walker House in East Quogue at the turn of the century. Through the latter part of the nineteenth century East Quogue was a teeming resort. Its many small, home-like summer boarding houses faced some competition when the huge Walker House went up. (East Quogue Historical Society Collection.)

*Jackson Ave., East Quogue, L. I.*

Jackson Avenue in East Quogue at the turn of the century. Many of the houses have survived, though the street name has been changed to Walker Avenue. (East Quogue Historical Society Collection.)

John G. Wendel's coach in Quogue, 1905. Bought from the Fifth Avenue Coach Company, the coach made several trips up and down Beach Lane for summer boarders during the 1890s and 1900s. Quogue began accommodating summer visitors shortly after railroad service reached Riverhead in 1844. Mr. Wendel's interests in Quogue included Quogue House, part of which is seen in the background. The landmark was razed in 1958. (Quogue Library Collection.)

The Howell House in Westhampton Beach in the early 1900s. In 1868, P.T. Barnum, one of Westhampton Beach's first summer visitors, convinced Mortimer Howell to build the Howell House, a summer hotel that lasted into the middle of this century. (Westhampton Beach Historical Society Collection.)

Quogue station in 1879. While welcomed as a boon to the boarding house business, the railway, which was extended through Eastport to Sag Harbor in 1870, was bitterly resented in Quogue. Sparks caused devastating forest fires and freight rates were high. No depot was built until local residents subscribed $1,000 in 1875 and then a dispute between the railroad authorities and the villagers over its location prompted the Long Island Rail Road to take draconian measures. Unhappy with the site the villagers had chosen for the station building, the LIRR instructed a crew to physically remove the structure. This they accomplished in the dead of night, dumping it in the woods near Riverhead Road. (Ron Ziel Collection.)

Jessup Avenue in Quogue, 1915. By 1915, the saddleries of the town's Main Streets had made way for automobile-related emporiums and parking spaces had become more important than hitching posts. In most other respects, Jessup Avenue remains much the same today as it was at the turn of the century. (Quogue Library Collection.)

The wreck of the *Augustus Hunt*, as recorded on film on January 22, 1904. A four-masted coaling schooner, the *Augustus Hunt* hit a sandbar and broke apart in heavy winds as surfmen from three life saving stations—Quogue, Potunk, and Tiana—struggled in vain throughout the stormy night to reach her crew. Frustrated by the continuing storm, accompanied by a heavy fog, they were able to save only two of the ship's crew. For their heroic rescues, surfmen William F. Halsey Jr. and Frank D. Warner received gold medals from the government. (Quogue Library Collection.)

Kate Blake in Quogue on July 4, 1905. The house that Miss Blake and her brother, Henry, built still stands on Ocean Avenue in Quogue. The two were early summer residents of the village. (Quogue Library Collection.)

The Hampton Inn in Westhampton Beach in the early 1900s. With its gambrel roof, its numerous rooms, its wide porch for rocking, and its carefully tended grounds, the Hampton Inn was the epitome of the summer boarding house at its biggest and best. (Westhampton Beach Historical Society Collection.)

The Clifton Hotel on Shinnecock Bay at the turn of the century. The Clifton Hotel, located on Lighthouse Road, was the largest of the boarding houses in Good Ground, now known as Hampton Bays. It could accommodate at least one hundred boarders who had at their disposal two tennis courts, thirty bath houses, and a long dock to stroll along. It burned down c. 1925. (Southampton Historical Museum Collection.)

Stefania Spiegel and Herman Grossman, c. 1905. When Joseph Fahys established his watchcase factory in Sag Harbor in 1881, the village economy got a significant boost as well as an infusion of new blood. Herman Grossman, one of many Jewish immigrants from Hungary where engraving had been developed into a high craft, was lured straight from the boat to Sag Harbor to etch delicate illustrations on watchcases. There, he met, courted, and married Stefania Spiegel, who had come to Sag Harbor from what was then Czechoslovakia to join her sister, the wife of Bernard Spitz.

Fahys watchcase factory, built in 1881. (John Jermain Library Collection.)

This bird's-eye view of Sag Harbor was taken in 1906. (Southampton Town Historian Collection.)

## Notice of Filing of Application.

In the Matter of the Final Application of

*George Michael Bury*

To be Admitted to Become a Citizen of the United States.

TO THE CLERK OF THE *Village* OF *Sag Harbor*

SIR: — Please take notice that I have made an application to be admitted to become a Citizen of the United States; that my full name is *George Michael Bury*; that my age is *43* years; that my occupation is *Watch Case maker*; that my residence is _____ in the *Village* of *Sag Harbor*; County of Suffolk, and State of New York, and that the name of the Court in which my petition has been filed and is pending is the *County* Court, Suffolk County.

Dated *June 8* 1904

*George M. Bury.*
(Petitioner's Signature.)

A notice of filing of application for citizenship, 1904. Many of the immigrants who found work in Sag Harbor at Joseph Fahys's watchcase factory hoped to become citizens and, like George Michael Bury, they filed applications that were signed by Cornelius R. Sleight. (John Jermain Library Collection.)

Our Lady of Poland Church in Southampton Village, 1919. In 1908, there were six Polish families in the area around Southampton Village; in 1910, there were twenty-nine. By 1918, 331 families of Polish origin in the area were traveling each Sunday by railroad, horse and buggy, and bicycle to St. Isidore's Church in Riverhead to attend Mass and it was decided that the time had come for a new parish to be established. Until the new church on Maple Street was completed, Mass was celebrated at Schwenk's Arcade on Main Street in Southampton. The first Mass in the new church was offered on Christmas Day, 1918, by the Reverend Alexander Cizmowski, pastor.

Konstanty Borkowski (left), and the Babinski brothers in the Borkowski corn fields, c. 1915. Most Polish immigrants who arrived in Southampton were farmers whose dream it was to own farms of their own. Many, including the Borkowski and Babinski families, achieved that goal and became successful farmers in the town.

58

The Konstanty Borkowski and Aleksandra Mierzejewska wedding party at Water Mill on May 15, 1915. Shown are, left to right: (back row) Czeslaw Jastrzebski (Chet Yastrzemski), Mr. Arnister (fiddler), Mr. Zebrowski, unknown, unknown, unknown, Ludwik Zaluska (Louis Thomas Zaluski) (fiddler), Mr. Stubelek (with his hands on the chair); (second row) unknown (with newspaper), Jozefa Mierzejewska Jastrzebska (Josephine Yastrzemski), Mrs. Grabowska, Mrs. Zebrowska, Stanislawa Borkowska Guzewicz (Stella Guzewicz) and daughter Celia Guzewicz Grubb, Mrs. Zebrowska, Mr. Zebrowski and son, Wincenty Zaluska (Vincent Zaluski), Jan Borkowski and son Francis Borkowski (Berkoski); (third row) Marcel Damiecki, Mrs. Zebrowska, Mr. Mitzkowski, Wladyslawa (Lena) Mierzejewska Poliksa Skripps, Konstanty Borkowski, Aleksandra Mierzejewska Borkowska (Alice Borkoski), Helen Borkowska Damiecki, Weronika Zaluska Borkowska (Veronica Zaluski Borkowski) and son Leo Borkowski (Borkoski), Anna Tyszka Zaluska (Anna Zaluski), and Stanislawa Zaluska Babinski (Stella Zaluski Babinski); (front row) John Zebrowski, Helen Zaluski Tiska, Janina Borkowska (Jean Berkoske), Helen Zebrowski, Helen Zebrowski (Yaphank), Anna Zebrowski, Thomas Yastrzemski, Jessie Zaluski, Alice Zaluski Bruzdoski, Bertha Zaluski Petty, and Martha Zaluski Taber.

Mary Byrne Brennan and family *c.* 1914. Mary Brennan, center with baby, and her husband Patrick arrived in Southampton from England via Boston and Orient Point in April of 1890. From 1901 to 1905 the family farmed in Mecox. When Patrick died in 1905, the family moved to Meeting House Lane in Southampton Village. Shown in this photograph are, left to right: (back row) Veronica Brennan (Nemier), William Brennan, Johanna Brennan (McGuirk), and Elizabeth Brennan (Schmitt); (front row) Edward McGuirk, Mary Byrne Brennan, baby Helen Nemier (Mercer), and Mary McGuirk (Bennett).

The Catholic church and rectory on Hill Street in Southampton Village, *c.* 1900. Built in 1892, this was the second Catholic church in the village, the first having been erected in 1881 in the area of the Hampton Road firehouse at the instigation of Mrs. Frederic H. Betts. Though she attended Saint Andrews Dune Church herself, arriving via gondola, she employed help who were Catholic and would not remain on the East End unless they were able to attend Sunday Mass. Neither building has survived. (Southampton Historical Museum Collection.)

The Methodist church and parsonage in Southampton Village, *c.* 1908. Identified as the Methodist Episcopal Church in a 1908 publication, the church served a congregation whose board of trustees first met in 1843, though Southampton had an established ministry long before the Revolution. For many years adherents met in various Southampton homes and were served by itinerant ministers. (Southampton Historical Museum Collection.)

The bank and the Presbyterian chapel in Westhampton Beach at the turn of the century. With their modest size and Queen Anne architectural influences, these structures were well suited to the needs and the aesthetic preferences of the era. The chapel was moved first to Library Avenue, then to Dune Road via water. It served as a residence there, then burned. (Westhampton Beach Historical Society Collection.)

Jobs Lane in Southampton Village, *c.* 1905. Though the road was as yet unpaved, the automobile had definitely arrived. These fine specimens line the south side of Jobs Lane in front of the J.S. Allen Automobile Repository, H.G. Squires's Automobile Garage, and Agawam Hall. (Southampton Town Historian Collection.)

Members of the Corwith and Foster families of Southampton Village in an early and very elegant automobile. (Southampton Historical Museum Collection.)

Machinists at the J.S. Allen Repository on Jobs Lane in Southampton Village, c. 1905. (Southampton Historical Museum Collection.)

The Bridgehampton to Sag Harbor "Scoot" in Sag Harbor, c. 1900. In 1870, tracks running through the woods from Bridgehampton to Sag Harbor were completed. The "Scoot" made a local run, meeting trains in Bridgehampton and taking passengers to Sag Harbor and back. The 5 miles of track were abandoned in May 1939. (Ron Ziel Collection.)

The "Scoot" in Eastport, c. 1910. Starting in 1870, the Long Island Rail Road ran a daily two-car train, from Amagansett to Greenport by way of Manorville, that was also known as the "Scoot." Its other nicknames were the "Cape Horn" because of its semicircular course, and the "Peanut Train" because of the paltry profits it brought the LIRR. The service was discontinued in 1931 and the Manorville tracks were torn out in 1949. (Ron Ziel Collection.)

The Hoyt house and the old mill at Shinnecock Hills, c. 1900. Having built the first summer home on the west bank of Lake Agawam in Southampton Village in 1872, Mr. and Mrs. William S. Hoyt went on to sell their village property and become the first to purchase property and build on Shinnecock Hills. Mrs. Hoyt, the daughter of Lincoln's Secretary of the Treasury, Salmon P. Chase, and a prominent cultural force in the village, bought the mill from its last owner, Thomas P. Warner. (Southampton Historical Museum Collection.)

A detail from a flier dating from c. 1900 promoting "Long Island's Little Art Village." The brainchild of the well-traveled Mrs. Hoyt, who had discovered "plein air" painting in Europe, the Shinnecock Summer School of Art was directed by the celebrated William Merritt Chase from 1891 to 1902. Concerned that Southampton lacked a level of culture worthy of its refined summer residents, Mrs. Hoyt enlisted two other summer residents, Mrs. Henry Kirke Porter and Samuel L. Parrish, to back the project. Mr. Parrish provided the land surrounding the school studio, which he divided and sold to various people who then built cottages on it. These cottages, together with the studio, came to be known as the Art Village, which has survived as a distinct and charming residential compound to this day.

Zella de Milhau on the porch at "Laffalot," her house in the Art Village, Shinnecock Hills, c. 1900. An amazing woman who drove one of the first automobiles in Southampton, organized the most talked-about social events, and generally stole the show wherever she went, Miss de Milhau was also a student at William Merritt Chase's summer art school. (Southampton Historical Museum Collection.)

Art Village cottages in Shinnecock Hills, c. 1900. "Laffalot," Zella de Milhau's cottage, is on the left. All the cottages were "low cut and grey shingled," according to a contemporary account, "none of them having been touched with paint . . .." (Southampton Historical Museum Collection.)

Students painting beside the road in Shinnecock Hills, *c.* 1900. The Shinnecock Summer School of Art, under the direction of the famously flamboyant William Merritt Chase, attracted some one hundred students a year. Mostly female, the aspiring artists were a familiar sight in the scrubby hills, which they sought to capture on canvas with the truth of expression and dashing vitality encouraged by the *maître*.

James Breese, c. 1910. James Breese bought 30 acres on Hill Street in 1895 and hired Stanford White to create a mansion in the style of Mount Vernon that was known as "The Orchard." Breese was an adventurous man who won and lost several fortunes, the last of which was lost in 1935. After selling "The Orchard" to Charles Merrill, he took a round-the-world trip before moving into a more modest house next to his former residence. In his seventies, he toured the country with a beautiful young companion/housekeeper/chauffeur who committed suicide when Mr. Breese died at the age of eighty. (Southampton Town Historian Collection.)

The south facade of "The Orchard" on Hill Street in Southampton Village. (Southampton Town Historian Collection.)

The music room at "The Orchard," *c.* 1910. When the vagaries of the stock market permitted, James Breese added to his Hill Street estate with the help of his friend, the architect Stanford White. In the music room, White's opulent tastes were reflected in the high, carved gilt columns, and in the painted Italian ceiling. The music room, undertaken in 1906, was probably White's last job; he was shot that summer. (Southampton Town Historian Collection.)

Samuel L. Parrish, c. 1910. Hailed as the "First Citizen of Southampton, LI." in his *New York Times* obituary in 1932, Samuel Parrish became a prominent landholder and patron of the arts in Southampton after he retired from his New York City law practice. He succeeded Albert J. Post as "president" of Southampton Village, where he founded the Parrish Art Museum and joined forces with his brother James in many other civic-minded projects. An active backer of the Rogers Memorial Library, he was also one of the organizers of the Shinnecock Hills Golf Club. A man in the patrician mold, he lived most of his life as a bachelor, marrying only late in life. He died in 1932 at the age of eighty-three. (Morris Studio Collection.)

The Rogers Memorial Library on Jobs Lane in Southampton Village in the 1890s. The library, designed by architect Robert H. Robertson, was made possible in 1895 by the will of Harriet Jones Rogers, who gave her Main Street home and $10,000 with which to found a village library. (Southampton Historical Museum Collection.)

Players on the course at Shinnecock Hills Golf Club in 1900. Samuel Parrish was among a small group of prominent men who founded the Shinnecock Hills Golf Club back when the game was new to sportsmen on this side of the Atlantic. The first twelve holes were completed by 1891, when it became the first course with a clubhouse to incorporate in this country. (Suffolk County Historical Society Fullerton Collection.)

Some women members of Shinnecock Hills Golf Club. Gathered in front of the clubhouse are the finalists in a 1901 women's tournament. The club's women were no duffers; for the first four years of its history (1895–1898), the United States Golf Association (USGA) women's title was in Shinnecock's possession. (Suffolk County Historical Society Fullerton Collection.)

The Meadow Club on First Neck Lane in Southampton Village, *c*. 1890. The club originated in the summer of 1879 with outdoor tea parties held by Mrs. Frederic H. Betts and her friend Mrs. Albert H. Buck in the meadow between their two houses. In 1887, the present site was bought and the club organized. By 1908 the club boasted thirty lawn tennis and two squash courts and remained open all winter so that off-season visitors, whose own homes were unheated, would have a warm place to stay.

Spectators at some Meadow Club matches, *c*. 1905. A few men were tieless but it was a rare woman who watched the tennis matches at the Meadow Club in 1905 wearing anything other than a pale summer dress and a hat. (Southampton Town Historian Collection.)

The Agawam Hotel in Southampton Village, c. 1910. Originally the Henry Culver house on the south side of Culver Hill, this handsome house with its mansard roof later operated year-round as the Agawam Hotel, though it was better known as Buchheit's. (Southampton Town Historian Collection.)

The Canoe Place Inn at Hampton Bays in the early 1900s. A stagecoach stop in the eighteenth century, Canoe Place has survived in many guises since then. It was owned by the Buchmullers (formerly of the Waldorf Astoria Hotel in Manhattan) in the early 1900s, when it attracted a fashionable clientele. Totally destroyed by a fire in 1921, it was rebuilt, along with several guest cottages, one of which Governor Alfred E. Smith occupied during the summer months for more than thirty years. (Morris Studio Collection.)

The bathing pavilion on Dune Road in Southampton Village, c. 1908. In the early days of the resort an organization known as the Southampton Bathing Association operated a bathing pavilion on the ocean beach just south of Lake Agawam. Equally popular with local and summer residents, it offered bathers "two able surfmen" on lifeguard duty and "230 separate bathing houses." In 1923 the era of democratic bathing ended when the Bathing Corporation of Southampton was organized to acquire the property and operations of the association. The Bathing Corporation operated as a private club and public facilities for ocean bathing were eventually provided further west at Cooper's Beach.

Terrell's Bathing Pavilion on Tiana Beach, c. 1900. No one looks ready for a dip despite the fact that this photograph is captioned "Heading for a swim." The man smoking a cigar at the right has been identified as Alonzo "Lonnie" Bellows by his daughter, Dr. Emma Bellows, the first female physician at Southampton Hospital. (East Quogue Historical Society Collection.)

Post's Bathing Beach in Quogue, 1910. Young men and children tackle the surf much as they do today, though without the surf mats and boards that came later. (Quogue Library Collection.)

The offices and staff of the *Sea-Side Times* on Southampton Village's Main Street, *c*. 1906. A predecessor and later a competitor of *The Southampton Press*, the *Sea-Side Times* was owned by Charles A. Jagger, the bearded man standing in the doorway of 38–40 Main Street. The lady on the extreme left is Hattie Havens (McAllister); third from left is Marie Rogers; and the boy on the extreme right is Bill Sayre. (Southampton Town Historian Collection.)

Five members of Southampton High School's 1909 girls' basketball team. (Southampton Historical Museum Collection.)

## Three

# Boomtime
# to Wartime

*In the early part of the century, the fashionable who flocked to Southampton's shores altered the economic as well as the physical landscape of the area. They not only built big houses and clubs for themselves, but many took a patrician interest in their adoptive villages as well. As local businesses prospered from the summer influx and as benefactors emerged from among the civic-minded newcomers, new public buildings and monuments mushroomed, roads were paved, rude railroad depots were replaced by elegant train stations, and the unpretentious resorts took on opulent airs. These were dampened—though hardly extinguished—by the imposition of the federal income tax in 1913 and the Great War, which broke out in Europe the following year.*

Main Street in Bridgehampton, 1910. Dedication ceremonies for the monument at the corner of Ocean Road and Montauk Highway were part of celebrations of the 250th anniversary of Bridgehampton's founding. The monument was conceived as a tribute to the sons of the village who died in three wars: 1776, 1812, and 1861. Other war dates were added later. (Bridge Hampton Historical Society Collection.)

"Tremedden" in Bridgehampton in the early 1900s. The era of the elaborate summer "cottage" began early in Bridgehampton, where fountain pen magnate Richard Esterbrook built "Tremedden" on the corner of Sagaponack Road and Ocean Road (then called Atlantic Avenue) over a five-year period from 1877 to 1882. In 1916, Charles Evans Hughes, who was running for president at that time, went to bed in this house on election night believing he had been elected, only to find the next morning that late returns from California gave the vote to Woodrow Wilson. "Tremedden," which is Welsh for "trees in the meadow," was torn down during the Great Depression when money for the upkeep of such a lavish estate was hard to come by. (Bridge Hampton Historical Society Collection.)

"Dolce Domum" in Bridgehampton in the early 1900s. "Dolce Domum" was built for Dr. John L. Gardiner in 1892. Hundreds of tons of local rock were used in the construction, which took two years to complete. From the tower, which still rises above the glacial moraine north of Bridgehampton, the doctor and his family had a view of Connecticut as well as of the Atlantic. (Bridge Hampton Historical Society Collection.)

A picnic on the grass, *c.* 1910. After Southampton became a busy summer resort, local families often sought refuge from the seasonal pressures in rustic "camps" built in the woods outside the villages. For Southampton's celebrated golf course designer, Seth Raynor (at the far right), The area known as West Neck was the place to escape the incessant telephone calls from Charles Blair MacDonald, the indefatigable Chicago Scotsman with whom Raynor collaborated on the National Golf Links of America, among other famous courses. Also enjoying the outing were Raynor's wife Mary Araminta Hallock Raynor (reclining in foreground); his wife's sister Gertrude Hallock Hildreth (in the black-banded hat); her husband James Augustus Hildreth (partially hidden), who served as Southampton Town Supervisor for 18 years; and Lizzie Burnett (also wearing a hat). The others, including the mischievous looking boy whistling into a bottle, remain unidentified.

Veronica Brennan (Nemier), left, and Elizabeth Brennan (Schmitt), c. 1910. The high-collared white dresses worn by the sisters were typical of the era.

Elizabeth Brennan (Schmitt) (left) and Ethel Shaver in 1917. Seven years after the photograph shown above was taken, skirts were still long but necks were revealed and fashion was clearly moving toward a new, less demure look.

Women of the Shinnecock Reservation, c. 1915. In an era when people dressed to travel, pay a call, or attend church, these women may have been headed for a shopping trip or a wedding in their finely worked outfits. Lillian Lee (Williams), left, and Mary Ann Lee (Hueston), right, flank their sister-in-law Edna (Kellis) Lee. Lillian Lee Williams' children living on the reservation today are Vivian Carle, Alice Franklin, Arthur T. Williams, Harry Williams, Caroline Bullock, and Donald Williams. Her sister's son, Lubin Hunter, and granddaughter, Roberta Hunter, are also Shinnecock residents.

Bridgehampton station, *c.* 1910. When the original rudimentary station building in Bridgehampton burned down in 1884, it was replaced with this handsome structure. This view shows the sawtooth canopy scalloping, the wood platform, and some of the common depot accessories of the day: a Fairbanks scale, a baggage handcart, and bicycles belonging to the station's staff. Though it was clearly deteriorating by the 1940s, this station was not torn down until 1964. (Ron Ziel Collection.)

Good Ground's second station, *c.* 1911. The simple structure that had served Good Ground (later Hampton Bays) since 1870 burned in 1873. The new, more imposing station was opened on January 10, 1874, on the east side of Ponquogue Avenue. (Ron Ziel Collection.)

Southampton Hose Company Number 1 members, c. 1911. More likely headed for a parade than a fire, company members include, left to right: Hugh Edwards, Peter Schug, Louis P. Schmitt, Maynard King, George Barr, Donald Bagshaw, Ernest Peterson, John W. Kampf, and James Davis.

Southampton Hospital, c. 1913. After making do in various buildings around town since its formation in 1909, Southampton Hospital was given property on Olde Towne Road in Southampton Village by Samuel L. Parrish in 1911. The gift of the property was contingent on the governors of the hospital building and maintaining an extension of Herrick Road, onto which the new hospital, designed by architect T. Markoe Robertson, would face.

The Windmill Lane School in Southampton Village at the turn of the century. Built in 1890, the Windmill Lane School was typical of a second wave of schools that went up when districts outgrew the basic one-room model that had served almost from the time of the first settlers. This was Southampton Village's only school, housing both the elementary and the high school. Later, after the construction of the Hampton Road School (now the town hall), the Windmill Lane building housed the first six grades. The old landmark was torn down in 1932. (Southampton Historical Museum Collection.)

A class at the Windmill Lane School in the early 1900s. (Southampton Historical Museum Collection.)

Third-graders on the steps of the Windmill Lane School, c. 1910. Twenty years after it was built, with mature greenery surrounding its foundation, the school stood less starkly on the high ground on the west side of Windmill Lane. Among those present for the class portrait are: Eleanor Howell (front row, fourth from the left); Mildred Eve (front row, sixth from the left); Ella Topping (front row, seventh from the left); and Elizabeth Hildreth (Johnson) (front row, ninth from the left). At the top, third from the left, is Hervey Topping.

Bridgehampton School on School Street in the early 1900s. This handsome structure served Bridgehampton students until 1930, when the present school on Montauk Highway was built. This photograph was taken looking north and it shows several residences that still stand on School Street. The Candy Kitchen had not yet replaced the corner building.

Hayground School, Montauk Highway and Hayground Road. This large, two-room schoolhouse with a belfry was built in 1912 on the site of two former, more modest, schools that served the once-distinct area between Water Mill and Bridgehampton known as Hayground. Considered very modern for its time, it had indoor plumbing and a coal-fired furnace that delivered steam heat. The Hayground Windmill, visible at right, was the last of the grist mills, driven by wind, to end operations. It was built in 1801.

Awaiting the train at Quogue, *c.* 1915. Automobiles were the conveyance of choice by 1915 and there were plenty of them lined up and waiting on Fridays when the weekenders arrived from New York. (Ron Ziel Collection.)

Paving North Main Street in Southampton Village, *c.* 1910. Sidewalks often came first but by the first decade of the twentieth century the task of paving Southampton Village's roads to accommodate the ever more popular automobile was well under way. (Southampton Historical Museum Collection.)

The Soldiers' and Sailors' Monument in Southampton Village, *c.* 1910. Begun in 1896, the monument was funded with $2,000 contributed by popular subscription and was designed and built under the supervision of General Thomas H. Barber. It was dedicated to the village in 1900 but actually completed in 1902. The guns, projectiles, and chains—the latter from an old sloop of war—were donated by the War and Navy Departments.

Sacred Hearts of Jesus and Mary Catholic Church in Southampton Village, 1912. This view shows the new church, built of marble from Dorset, Vermont, shortly after its completion in 1908. At the time, the building to the right served as the rectory and the old church as a parish hall. The residence at the extreme right was a convent. Only the new church remains today.

A pageant at Agawam Park in Southampton Village on June 12, 1915. Important anniversaries of Southampton's founding have always been occasions for huge, community-wide celebrations, though they have become less frequent than they once were. In 1915, to commemorate the town's 275th anniversary, a particularly memorable series of events was held, including a pageant, in which costumed participants portrayed in dramatic form the highlights of Southampton's history. This group represented the Native American population that preceded the first Europeans and helped them survive. Among them are Elizabeth Hildreth (Johnson) in the front row, second from the left, and her sister Mary Araminta (Greenfield) to her left.

Some members of the Shinnecock tribe and others depicted a Shinnecock scene at the 275th anniversary pageant. (Southampton Historical Museum Collection.)

A group of costumed participants in the 1915 pageant. (Southampton Historical Museum Collection.)

Agawam Hall on Jobs Lane in Southampton Village, *c.* 1910. Built in 1890, Agawam Hall was a combination roller-skating rink and theater. It had a broad floor with movable seats and an elevated stage and was frequented by both summer and local residents. The Honorable Elihu Root (who was appointed secretary of state in 1905), Charles Evans Hughes, and many others filled its hall with their oratory. Singers from the Metropolitan performed there, as did Gentleman Jim Corbett, Mrs. Tom Thumb, and numerous minstrel troupes. Plays were performed on its stage and an early form of moving pictures generated by the hand-cranked Robertson's Projectoscope were seen there. In about 1915, however, progress outpaced its offerings, and Agawam Hall was demolished. (Southampton Historical Museum Collection.)

Members of an acrobatic act in Southampton Village, *c.* 1920. Jim Marran, who served on the police force in real life, is the man with the moustache in this portrait of players who performed locally.

Local talent on the boards in Southampton Village, *c.* 1920. Jim Marran is the third man from the left in this wood-cutting skit.

A scene on Jobs Lane, *c.* 1915. The H.G. Squires Automobile garage and Agawam Hall stood next to each other on the south side of Jobs Lane in Southampton Village. Frank Nemier is the

Squires employee identified with a cross.

The "Old Sayre House" on Main Street in Southampton Village being razed in 1912. Built in 1648 by Thomas Sayre, one of the eight original founders of the Southampton colony, the Sayre house stood on Main Street until it was thought to be the oldest wooden building on the American continent and possibly in the world. In 1912 it was condemned as a fire hazard and torn down, and thus one of the last reminders of the seventeenth-century village was eliminated. The brick building on the left is the village hall. (Southampton Town Historian Collection.)

The interior of the First National Bank of Southampton in the early 1900s. Before the splendid new bank building was completed in 1912 on the corner of Main and Cameron Streets in Southampton Village, the bank operated on the east side of Main Street at Wall Street. In fact, it was the bank's location that is said to have given Wall Street its name suggestive of high finance. (Morris Studio Collection.)

Bay beach in Southampton in the 1920s. Bay beaches like Still's on the Peconic in Shinnecock Hills and North Sea in Southampton featured elaborate floats and pavilions and were festive all summer long. (Morris Studio Collection.)

The Irving House in Southampton Village. A twelve-room boarding house around 1870, by the turn of the century the Irving House was well on its way to becoming the imposing sixty-three-bedroom hotel that catered to wealthy and socially prominent patrons for decades. One of Southampton's best-known landmarks, the rambling wooden structure was considered obsolete in 1974 when it was torn down and its contents sold at auction.

The *Clan Galbraith*, aground near Flying Point in July 1916. Everyone wanted to take a look at the beached four-masted bark from Norway after it went aground near Flying Point on July 22, 1916. It went ashore so high on the beach that people could walk to it.

Hunters, *c.* 1915. The waters around Sag Harbor, as elsewhere in the town, were once a gunner's paradise, as this shot of five duck-laden local sportsmen attests. (John Jermain Library Collection.)

Young Southampton Village patriots belonging to the Southampton Rifle Military Group in a portrait taken when the Great War was on everyone's mind. In the back row, third from the right, is Edward Brennan; fifth from the right is William Brennan; and seventh from the right is Joseph Brennan. All three Brennans fought in World War I and all three returned to resume their lives. Edward, who later served as mayor of Southampton Village, re-enlisted to fight in World War II, and finished his military career in the navy as a commander. William was an army private and Joseph a navy ensign. Joseph Quinlan also appears in the portrait.

A 1917 photograph of Southampton Village resident Louis Schmitt in his World War I army uniform.

Elizabeth Brennan Schmitt and her husband, Louis, in 1919. Just out of the army, Southampton Village resident Louis Schmitt and his new bride are packed for their wedding trip up the Hudson.

World War I veterans on parade on Main Street in Southampton Village, c. 1920. (Southampton Historical Museum Collection.)

A wartime scene in Southampton Village. During and after World War I, scenes such as this were enacted all over the country as villages like Southampton honored native sons returned from the front. (Southampton Historical Museum Collection.)

Southampton High School's championship 1919 football team. The players are, left to right: (front row) Louis Ginachio, Frank McLaughlin, Captain George Whitby, Carlton Streit, Charles Corrigan, and John Glick; (back row) Coach Henriquez, Zeke Halsey, Edgar Donnelly, Wendell "Oscar" Phillips, Henry Baird, Ben Rosen, and Carlton Reeves.

Richard G. Hendrickson at the family farm in Bridgehampton in 1918. Mr. Hendrickson's father was the last to farm commercially on Gardiner's Island, the 3,300-acre quasi-fiefdom in Gardiner's Bay granted to the Gardiner family by King Charles I in 1639. During the great influenza epidemic of 1918/19, young Richard spent the summer out of harm's way on the idyllic island and returned home with a wooly companion.

The dedication of the American Legion Building in Southampton Village, 1929. Suitably scheduled for the Fourth of July, the dedication of the legion's new headquarters brought veterans, clergymen, and prominent members of Southampton Village society together for the ceremonies. Shown in his uniform, fourth from the right, is Dr. David H. Hallock. (Southampton Town Historian Collection.)

Split Rock in the early 1900s. One local landmark that will probably never be sacrificed on the altar of progress is Split Rock in Water Mill. (Southampton Historical Museum Collection.)

# Four

# Into the
# Twentieth Century

*Through two world wars and the Great Depression, Southampton held to its agricultural roots and remained a summer haven for the affluent who escaped the worst economic effects of this era. No one was immune from the devastating impact of the 1938 hurricane, however, in which many mansions and prominent Southampton landmarks were lost. While many others have since disappeared in the rush of post-war development, community pride and preservationist sentiment are strong in Southampton, which still boasts beautiful vistas of open spaces and farmland, wide beaches, and leafy village streets.*

The dedication of Southampton Town Hall, c. 1925. The building at the northwest corner of Hampton Road at Main Street in Southampton Village was later converted for retail use. (Southampton Town Historian Collection.)

The National Golf Links of America clubhouse in Shinnecock Hills, overlooking Peconic Bay, c. 1920. Charles Blair MacDonald, an American who had attended St. Andrews in Scotland and one of the early giants of the game, conceived of a course for Southampton that would present the supreme test of golf. Seth Raynor, a civil engineer from Southampton who had been responsible for much of the village's public works, laid out the course around 1907 on property that founders purchased for $40,000 in Sebonac. The magnificent Georgian-style clubhouse, built by Donnelly and Corrigan of Southampton, is still in use; Seth Raynor went on to design courses in many parts of the world. (Morris Studio Collection.)

The D.A.R. float in the 1923 Fourth of July parade. The war had been won, summer stretched ahead, and there was much to celebrate at the annual Fourth of July parade in Southampton Village. Richard Fowler was at the wheel; Adelaide Corwith was a proud "Liberty," bearing the flag. The others are, from left to right: Natalie Howell, Clarice Phillips, Amanda Ruland, Mrs. R. M. Corwith, Madeline Blackburn, Dorothy Schwenk, and Edna Elliston. (Southampton Historical Museum Collection.)

J. Earle Stevens Jr., pictured in July 1921. Dapperly dressed, young Master Stevens arrived at the beach on Dune Road in Southampton in princely style, driving his "Red Bug."

Grace and Mae Collins, *c.* 1920. The Collins sisters were the image of carefree youth in the twenties as they modeled the latest in bathing costumes.

Louis Schmitt, right, and a friend, *c.* 1920. Suits might be single-breasted, double-breasted, striped or not, but collars were still high and hats were seldom absent when Louis Schmitt of Southampton Village was a young man.

Shinnecock Hills station in 1923. Developer Austin Corbin built this turreted structure in 1887 as a station and a real estate sales office. He and a group of New York investors had formed the Long Island Improvement Company and purchased the hills (3,200 acres) in the 1880s. The station, which commanded a sweeping view of the then-barren hills, served as a train stop until the late 1930s. Corbin's company went bankrupt in 1893 and he died in 1896, but the mail was still picked up by train and the building continued to function as a post office even when trains no longer stopped there. By 1973, the station was boarded up and abandoned but is has since been salvaged as a private home. (Ron Ziel Collection.)

A Halsey and White truck and crew in the 1920s. The purchase of a new truck at Halsey and White, the predecessor to Southampton Coal and Produce (which is still in business on North Main Street in Southampton Village) was an occasion worthy of capturing on film. Standing in front of the company's latest acquisition are, from left to right: William Henry Martin, Garland Gill, and his brother Waverly Gill.

The Stachecki family of Southampton Village in 1924. Waclaw Stachecki (in the back row with his sons Chester and Stanley) came to this country from Poland in 1912. His wife, Josephine, holding baby Anelia, came a year later. After stopping in Brooklyn, then working for farmers in Wainscott, Mr. Stachecki acquired farmland of his own in Southampton on the southwest side of the intersection of County Road 39 and Hampton Road, where his wife opened the first farmstand in the area. Standing next to their mother are Floryan and Helen, and seated in front are Martha and Walter.

Members of the Picnic Club of Southampton Village in the 1920s. Organizations like the Picnic Club flourished in the early part of the century when commercial entertainments were few and restaurants reserved for very special occasions. Shown in the front row, from left to right, are: Bess Green, Clara Corwith, Miss Julia, Gertrude Hildreth, Mrs. Hugh Halsey, and Susan Hildreth. Included in the back row are: Mame Rogers, Charlotte Fordham, Grace Ellsworth, Lilys Post, and Nell Ives.

The Sunrise Trail Band aboard the steamer *Shinnecock, c.* 1925. The Long Island Rail Road was much more than a transportation company in its heyday. It played an active role in promoting tourism and even had its own band, which entertained travelers and burnished the railroad's image. (Ron Ziel Collection.)

Seventh-graders at the Hampton Road School in 1930. After sixty-six years, Harry Martin, shown at the far right of the second row from the top, remembers every classmate. Harry's classmates in 1930 were, left to right: (front row) Francis Cambria, Walter Guldi, Frank Campbell Austin, Arthur McGowan, Robert Havens, and Leo Zaloga; (second row) Mildred Miller, Margaret Bradley, Helen Bishop, Dorcas Cameron, Ethel Crutchley, Ruth Edwards, Fleurette Guilloz, and Mary Corwin; (third row) Olive Elizabeth Smith, Emily VanBrunt, Shirley Feinberg, Eunice Harris, Helen Goleski, Dorothy Johnson, and Bessie Silver; (fourth row) Douglas Morris, Abraham Frank, Howard Doering, Robert Miller, Zigmund Sokoloski, Henry Hildreth, and Harry Martin; (fifth row) John McGowan, Peter Wilson, Bob "Red" Ellsworth, Henry "Hank" Beckman, Alec Dunkirk, Chester Kominski, and Eugene Halsey.

A group at the Vacation Bible School at Bethel Presbyterian Church (now Gideon Lodge) in Southampton Village, c. 1930. The teacher, Miss Benjamin (standing), is flanked by Lewis Martin on the left and Harry Martin and Grant Ashman on the right. Seated, from left to right, are: Lilly Jasper, Evelyn Grigg, Annie Gill, and Ruth Bailey.

Members of the Southampton High School Band pictured around 1935. In high school, Harry Martin played in the band, almost every member of which he is able to identify. Among the musicians who were directed by band leader Jesse Lillywhite and band major Robert Aldrich (not in photograph) are: (seated) Harriet White, Florence Halsey, George Hudson, Constance Edwards, Isaura Frankenbach, Bob Malmros, Joe Bradley, James Halsey, Clarice Phillips, twins Maria and Alma Ivarone, Arlene Austin, Norma Malmros, Norman Sandford, Alfred Koral, Harry Martin, John Singleton, Emil Norsic, Hans Wobst, Harriet Sandford, Julia Robinson, Shirley Brown, Paul Liehr, and Millicent Cameron; (standing) Norman Lane, Abraham Halsey, William Glanville, Audrey Schwenk, Elaine Fairbanks, Miss Meschutt, Harold Feinberg, Margaret Smith, Edgar Phillips, Peter Wolf, Sam Herrick, Jimmy Halsey, Betty Palmer, Stephen Micari, Ray Blydenburgh, Charlie Halsey, Ernie Marshall, Frank Crippen, Dorcas Cameron, Joseph Wozniak, Walter Guldi, Gilbert Carter, Billy Nugent, and Raymond Enstine.

The Quantuck Yacht Club dock in Quiogue, c. 1930. Fine weekends still find the waters around Westhampton Beach liberally sprinkled with sails. The Quantuck dock has been the starting point for many a race. (Westhampton Beach Historical Society Collection.)

S.S. boats on Quantuck Bay, Westhampton Beach, in the 1930s. The S.S. design was highly favored by young people in Westhampton Beach, who raced regularly on Quantuck Bay. Number 105 belonged to the Maynards in the thirties and forties, when Jane Niebrugge raced number 121. (Westhampton Beach Historical Society Collection.)

Brouwer's Castle (later the Casa Basso restaurant) in Westhampton in the 1930s. Built around the turn of the century by the potter Theophilus Brouwer, an eccentric whose work is still highly prized, the castle, with its two musketeers and other fantastic statuary, has been the site of a restaurant since the early 1930s. (Westhampton Beach Historical Society Collection.)

The "Fishermen's Special" in the 1930s. For years, the Long Island Rail Road ran a special train for fishing enthusiasts. It left Pennsylvania Station in the wee hours of the morning and made just two stops, arriving towards dawn at the Shinnecock Canal and continuing on to Montauk. The service was discontinued in the 1960s. (Morris Studio Collection.)

The "South Shore Express" at the Shinnecock Canal on June 13, 1931. In June 1931, a new railroad bridge replaced a lighter bridge, which was not strong enough for the heavy locomotives the Pennsylvania Railroad was ready to put into service. On June 13, the "South Shore Express" was the last train to cross the old bridge before the new one was swung into place in just three hours. (Ron Ziel Collection.)

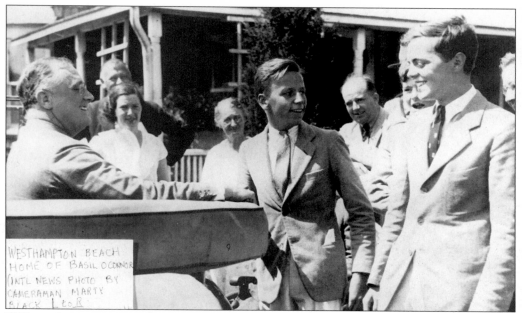

FDR on the campaign trail in Westhampton Beach in 1932. At the home of Basil O'Connor, photographer Marty Black caught the moment when Franklin Delano Roosevelt shook young Jay Rutherfurd's hand. Stewart Preston (right) appears to be next. (Southampton Town Historian Collection.)

A 1930s Fourth of July parade in Southampton Village. Representatives of the Polish-American Political Club of Southampton came out in impressive numbers for the annual patriotic parade.

The Whaler's Church (Presbyterian) on Union Street in Sag Harbor sometime before 1938. Attributed to Minard Lafever, the church was built in 1843/44 during the peak era of Sag Harbor's wealth. The steeple, shaped like a sailor's spyglass, was 187 feet tall and was a great source of pride in the village until the winds of the 1938 hurricane lifted it spectacularly straight up in the air, swung it clear of the building, and dropped it, smashing it to smithereens. It has never been replaced, though there is a movement attempting to do so. (Southampton Town Historian Collection.)

The westward view from the Southampton Bathing Corporation on Dune Road in Southampton Village. This photograph was taken before the hurricane of 1938. The Bathing Corporation swimming pool is in the foreground and, still standing next door, are the original public bathing station and bath houses.

Spectators looking over the remains of the public bath houses on Dune Road after the 1938 hurricane. The hurricane that struck the town on September 21, 1938, altered the landscape more than any other single event in the town's history.

The view from West Bay Bridge in Westhampton Beach on September 21, 1938, after the hurricane. The "eye" of the hurricane passed directly over Westhampton Beach and it was in that vicinity that the toll of death and destruction reached its height, though villages throughout the town were hard hit. Spectators were out within hours to survey the flattened dunes and the remains of West Bay Bathing Pavilion (later the Swordfish Club).

Westhampton Beach on September 21, 1938. The mingled bay and ocean rose to unprecedented heights during the hurricane, completely flooding Main Street in Westhampton Beach and reaching Montauk Highway. Boats like this one, and even large yachts, were left high and dry or splintered, along with home furnishings and remnants of wrecked buildings.

Henry W. Adelwerth (at left, aged sixteen) and his brother Vitus Adelwerth in Speonk, *c.* 1939. The Adelwerth brothers are shown in front of the business they opened on Montauk Highway in Speonk. The building, diagonally across from the present post office, is now a small residence. The business expanded and moved to its present location on Montauk Highway in Eastport. Called Adelwerth Bus Service, it has taken hundreds of children to and from schools throughout eastern Suffolk County over the years.

A whale ashore in 1944. Once fairly common, this is a sight almost never seen nowadays. (Southampton Historical Museum Collection.)

A Colonial wedding party in Southampton Village's 1940 pageant. The tricentennial pageant was an elaborately choreographed extravaganza in which most of the village participated.

Iceboating on Mecox in the 1940s. Mention of iceboating was made as early as 1837 by a Water Mill man and it has been a favorite activity for farmers and fishermen with time to spare in winter since that date. Significant improvements in design have been made over the years and iceboats are known to attain speeds in excess of 60 miles an hour. Regular races are still held on weekends whenever there is ice.

Flooded farmland in Bridgehampton in the 1940s. When farming was mechanized after World War II, small fields, often bordered by hedgerows, gave way to huge, sweeping fields. The runoff was apt to cause flooding as it did here at the Hendrickson farm on Lumber Lane.

Alfred E. Smith and Nicholas Murray Butler at the Southampton Bathing Corporation, c. 1940. Columbia University President Nicholas Murray Butler (right) might have been discussing trends in men's styles with his equally dapper friend and former New York State Governor Alfred E. Smith. (Southampton Town Historian Collection.)

The Reverend William H. Green with his wife, Josephine, in the 1940s. After the land was secured for the First Baptist Church in Southampton Village and the new church was erected on Halsey Avenue, the Reverend William H. Green came as pastor to Southampton, where he met and married his wife Josephine. The car behind the couple is a Duesenberg.

Women of the Red Cross in Southampton Village, *c.* 1942. When Southampton men went to fight in World War II, the women filled in on the home front. Here, Red Cross volunteers familiarize themselves with the workings of the internal combustion engine at Smyzer's garage. Elliott Smyzer is the man with the hat; Bob Hedges is hatless. Janet Jordan is seated behind the barrel of motor oil. Also at work are: Harriet Vail, Elsie Dunwell, Charlotte Cord, Priscilla Hildreth, Helen Finson, Marjorie Blythe (leaning over motor), and Winnie Willer. (Southampton Town Historian Collection.)

The Cooper's Beach bus in the early 1940s. When World War II brought gas rationing and other scarcities, a bus took village children to Southampton Village's public beach at the end of Cooper's Neck Lane. (Southampton Historical Museum Collection.)

Douglas Carle and William Bess at the Shinnecock Reservation School, *c.* 1945. Shinnecock children attended this one-room schoolhouse through the eighth grade until it burned not long after this picture was taken. Thereafter they attended school in the village.

The White Eagles, c. 1947. Winners of the Sunrise League in 1935, the White Eagles provided an extraordinary example of Polish prowess on the diamond. The local league included teams from East End locales and took its baseball seriously, as evidenced by the phenomenal success of the boy seated in front with the bats, Carl Yastrzemski Jr. Then an elementary school student in Bridgehampton, he went on to play with the Red Sox and to win the Triple Crown in 1967. Behind him are, left to right: (kneeling) Carl Yastrzemski, Sr. (Carl Jr.'s father, who had played in the semi-pros), Stanley Yastrzemski, Alex Borkoski, Chet Yastrzemski, and Raymond Yastrzemski; (back row) Mr. Jasinski, the Skoniezny brothers, a Jasinski brother, "Brownie" Emilita, and Raymond Andrews.

Wilmun "Billy" Halsey at the duck farm owned by his grandfather, Chester Raynor, on Tanner's Neck Lane in Westhampton, c. 1943. In the 1940s, more than six million ducks, or about half of all the ducks in the United States, were produced annually in Suffolk County. In the years since then, most of the duck farms in the town have been sold as valuable waterfront property. (Westhampton Beach Historical Society Collection.)

The demolition of the Ponquogue Lighthouse in 1948. The 170-foot Ponquogue, or Shinnecock, Lighthouse was built on the mainland in 1858 at approximately the halfway point between the Montauk and Fire Island Lighthouses. It was superseded and taken out of service in 1931 and then demolished, despite the efforts of preservationists to save it, on December 23, 1948.